Joy to the World
The Cram Family Christmas Cards

by

M. Regina Cram

For information regarding permission, contact the author, Regina Cram, at mregina.cram@gmail.com:

Cram, M. Regina
Joy to the World: The Cram Family Christmas Cards

ISBN: 979-8-9990339-0-1

Printed in the U.S.A.
First American edition, October 2025

Acknowledgments

I am profoundly grateful to my parents, the late Patricia Petrilli and Herbert Waite, my sisters, Virginia Martin and the late Marietta Tierney Waite, as well as two stepfathers, the late Mike Gradone and Hank Petrilli (It's a long story).

Thanks to Mirja Johanson, to whom, by tradition, I mail the first Christmas card each year. I have everlasting love for lifetime friends Pat Peck, Carla Ruiz, Marilyn Nelson, Betsy Myers and Nancy Wilber. As always, I thank my children, Peter (Skip) Jr. and Kaitlyn Cram, Meredith and Chris Dresko, Tierney and Andrew Keogler, Victoria (Torrie) and Mike Lalime, and our bonus Cram, Libby Martin, as well as the new generation who bring me joy and laughter.

I thank my husband, Peter, who loves me for who I am – not for who I probably should be.

Most of all, I thank God. Not sure what else I can say about Him. He rocks.

Dedication

for Peter
Did I ever tell you you're my hero?

Joy to the World

The Cram Family Christmas Cards

Introduction

It began with defeat. For several years we'd been sending those bland boxed Christmas cards that are as appealing as soggy cardboard. I yearned for the personalized Christmas cards of my childhood – the ones we designed ourselves. Growing up, my artistic mother would create a sketch for the cover of the family Christmas card. Occasionally she delegated the task to one of my sisters or me, with charming results. My father would write really bad poetry for the inside – so bad it was funny. They'd bring it to a local printer and – *voila!* – family Christmas cards.

I wanted to make cards like that, but it was out of the question. I have the artistic talent of a Popsicle and I'm terrible at writing in verse. I was defeated before I began.

Gradually, however, an idea began to take shape. Who says the inside of a Christmas card needs to be in rhyme? Why not write a story about something that happened in our lives that year? I'm not talking about the Suzy-goes-to-Harvard-Johnny-is-a-Rhodes-Scholar sort of thing. I prefer everyday stories about everyday life. And our children could be the illustrators.

That first year, I asked 4-year-old Skip to draw a picture of Mary, Joseph and Jesus in the stable at Bethlehem. He enthusiastically set to work with paper and markers. His drawing of Mary was hilarious; she was so tall she didn't fit inside the stable. The best part was the gorilla next to the sheep and oxen.

Unfortunately the drawing became badly smudged. This was before the era of Photoshop, so I reluctantly asked Skip to draw the Nativity picture again. Alas, this one had no gorilla in the mist – and no amount of coaxing could induce Skip to add it.

I wrote a funny story about our young children playing with the creche. I found a hole-in-the-wall print shop to create the cards (cheaper than boxed cards), and reticently mailed them to 75 friends and family. I'd never seen a card like ours and had no idea how it would be received. I only hoped people wouldn't think it silly.

I needn't have been concerned. The response was enthusiastic, which encouraged me to do it again the following year, and the year after that. It's not uncommon for people to contact us during the year just to confirm they're still on our Christmas-card list.

So here are 36 years of our family Christmas cards, from 1989 to 2024. I've also included never-before-seen cards that got voted down by the family. I call them Failures and Rejects.

1989 – Gorillas for Jesus

When we first set up our hardy wooden creche last year, we began finding it surrounded by creatures not found in Bethlehem. Our daughter Meredith, then 2½, loved to intermingle three plastic dinosaurs alongside the sheep, oxen and camels. She also kept stealing the Baby Jesus and hiding Him at the bottom of her Christmas stocking.

Not to be outdone, 4-year-old Skip assembled hordes of tiny rubber musclemen, positioning them like miniature bouncers around the stable.

In July, the kids begged to set it up again. Why not? The Nativity story is for always, not just Christmas. This time Skip brought out his G.I. Joe attack jet. It was a gift from a friend who, knowing our dislike of toy guns, thoughtfully gave him instead a war plane armed with 16 miniature bombs. Skip insisted he was not bombing the Holy Family; he was protecting Jesus from bad guys.

This Christmas surely we will see the addition of Teenage Mutant Ninja Turtles, complete with green slime, as well as our young daughter Tierney scampering to gum to death any sheep she can get her hands on.

We love watching them play. We're reminded that as a grown man, Jesus called out for the children to come to Him, and we stand in awe of our God, before whom, ultimately, every creature will bow.

Maybe even little rubber musclemen.

Merry Christmas with love,
Peter, Regina
Skip, Meredith and Tierney Cram

1990 – Questions

"If Santa Claus visits all children everywhere, why are there children in the world who have no toys?"

This question, posed by our 5-year-old philosopher, pierced the tranquility of our Christmas preparations.

Meredith, our resident 4-year-old humanitarian, listened in as we gingerly discussed poverty, thankfulness and generosity.

Other questions followed.

Does God love bad guys? Why doesn't Big Bird live with a grown up? Do I have Jesus living in my heart? What color is my skin? Why didn't anyone want Jesus born at their house? And our favorite: When I lie down, does the God who lives in my heart get to lie down too, or does He have to stay standing up?

Such curiosity, such willingness to include simple truths into their lives. Isn't that part of the miracle of Christmas, that God left the distant heights to live among us? Meredith caught a glimpse of this when she handed me a small figurine and said, "Mama, will you take care of Baby Jesus for a little while? Mary and Joseph are going on a date."

May such childlike faith be part of all of us this holiday season.

Merry Christmas!
Peter and Regina Cram
Skip, Meredith and Tierney

1991 – Gratitude

Christmas packages waiting to be opened: That's how 5-year-old Meredith sees life, with the most (and the biggest) parcels reserved for herself, of course. Meredith takes it for granted that Christmas will come, just as she takes it for granted that Daddy will make it home from work tonight, that babies are born healthy, that the Red Sox will lose.

So did we, until a near-tragedy shook our world. On July 31 this year, we welcomed a delightful new life – Louise Victoria – and nearly lost Regina in the process. During those terrible days when life hung in the balance, many things became clearer. Faith in God is important; impressing the boss is not. A loving marriage is precious while a new BMW is worthless.

In the aftermath of such a crisis, we find ourselves changed. We're not as likely to get bent out of shape when a driver cuts us off or annoyed when kids leave dirty socks on the floor. Loved ones are more cherished. Donuts taste better. And for all of this, we are overwhelmingly thankful to God!

It is, of course, the same God who graced us with His Son at a price which, this summer, we were all too grateful to not have to pay: life itself. Perhaps this Christmas you will share our gratitude for all God's blessings. After all, loved ones do not always make it home safely at night. If yours did, thank God for it.

Merry Christmas!
Peter and Regina Cram
Skip, Meredith, Tierney and Victoria

1992 – Bad Guys R Us

Within this picture-book home lurks a terror shared by children everywhere: bad guys. Our children have a bizarre fascination with this underbelly of life. Skip, our 8-year-old philosopher, wants to understand the cosmic significance of bad guys. Why did God make them? How can God love bad guys if they do bad things? Meredith, 6½, battles her fear of them by closing her curtains and praying for protection. Tierney, nearly 4, wants to know the nitty-gritty stuff, like whether bad guys wear socks. She has developed the rather ingenious theory that there are *good* bad guys and *bad* bad guys. Only *bad* bad guys do 'bad fings' but they are all locked in jail, so she is safe. Victoria, at 16 months, is oblivious to these weighty concerns as long as we feed her from time to time and allow her an occasional room to dismantle.

There's a truth about bad guys that our children don't fully understand: They're not just the other guy. It's why we are celebrating Christmas in the first place: An innocent baby – the only true Good Guy – came among us to save us from the ultimate bad guy. Fortunately for all of us, this is one Good Guy who wins in the end. So celebrate with us!

Merry Christmas,
Peter and Regina Cram
Skip, Meredith, Tierney and Victoria

1993 – The Lost Sheep

It was a warm autumn day when tragedy befell our family: Susannah got lost. Tierney's beloved stuffed bunny used to have rugged good looks and firm definition; but, like many of us, she became gray and balding and her stuffing bunched around the middle. We looked everywhere for Susannah, turning the house upside down and searching the neighborhood in torrential rain, without success.

Poor Tierney was heartsick. That's why she loves the story of the lost sheep. A farmer has 100 sheep and, when one wanders off, the farmer searches until he finds it. Then he throws a big party to celebrate. One day Tierney asked, "Why did the farmer go after the sheep? He still had all those other sheeps." I asked if she thought we'd search for her if she got lost; after all, we'd still have three kids left.

She was shocked and shouted, "Yes! Because you love me!" Her eyes glistened as we assured her that we'd never, ever stop looking until we found her. "Then would we have a party?" she pressed. "A big party? With cake?"

And so it was a party was held for a lumpy stuffed bunny who was found after three weeks deep inside a closet. Susannah even shared her cake with Tierney ("because Susannah's not too hungry tonight"). And now, one 4-year-old understands something of God's great love and the lengths to which He goes to reach us... like torrential rain, or birth in a cold Christmas stable.

Merry Christmas,
Peter and Regina Cram
Skip, Meredith, Tierney and Victoria

1994 – Childish Prayers

A child's prayer is the ultimate in sweetness, isn't it? Yeah, right. Like the time Tierney prayed for her baby sister to move in with the neighbors, preferably for a very long time. Skip's first prayer asked God to protect his Play-Doh from the clutches of baby Meredith. Years ago when I misplaced my wedding ring, young Skip prayed confidently to find it, then whispered his back-up plan. "That's okay, Mama. You get married again, get another ring."

Our children have asked God to make the Tooth Fairy less forgetful, turn the green beans into chocolate, and send all mosquitoes to Rhode Island. Torrie routinely thanks God for her sneakers. Meredith once thanked God for the baby's slimy belly button and asked Him to be sure there are no frogs in heaven. Skip prayed for quadruplet brothers. We drew the line when one unidentified child asked God if He could please make the teacher sick for the rest of the school year.

Children's prayers are not always sweet, or even kind, but they are genuine pleas from kids who understand that God cares about the details of our lives. After all, Christmas is a celebration of His coming among us because He cares so much, right? So maybe praying about green beans and frogs isn't so crazy. And maybe Rhode Islanders ought to be getting a little nervous right about now.

Merry Christmas!

Peter and Regina Cram

Skip, Meredith, Tierney and Victoria

1995 – The Twins

The confusion began innocently enough when we bought our first creche. The wooden stable came with animals, wise men and Baby Jesus, but no parents or shepherds. (It was on sale.) Our kids were understandably upset that the poor Baby was left to fend for Himself, so we designated the wise men as Mary, Joseph and a friend.

Years later, we received a beautiful handmade set from my sister Ginny, mother of six and artistic queen of Texas. Combined, they make a spectacular nativity. We have a real Mary and Joseph, six wise men, two shepherds, plenty of bleating sheep, and one big problem: We have twin Baby Jesuses.

We didn't realize the 3-year-old was confused until she told a friend Christmas is a birthday party for the Jesus twins. We tried explaining there's actually only one Jesus, and the 6-year-old clarified it was sort of like having two different Barbie dolls. The 3-year-old remained unconvinced.

Several years have passed for the only family in Glastonbury with Jesus Twins. Then last week we overheard the kids talking. "Christmas is coming soon!" the 4-year-old exclaimed. "That means we all get presents because it's Jesus's birfday! And we get to sing Happy Birfday to Jesus!"

"But there's only one Jesus, you know," the resident know-it-all explained with an air of superiority. "Don't get confused just because we have two of them in our living room."

"Everybody knows *that*!" the 4-year old replied in disgust.

Maybe I was wrong about the confusion. They seem to understand pretty well what Christmas is all about.

Merry Christmas!
Peter and Regina Cram
Skip, Meredith, Tierney and Torrie

M. Regina Cram

1996 – Unconditional Love

It was a hot summer day at the post office as I juggled parcel, baby, purse and the grip of two preschoolers. We were mailing a care package to a state prison where my sister Marietta was an inmate.

That's when 3-year Meredith piped up. "Mama?" she asked in that sweet voice of innocence. "Is Auntie Etta a bad guy?" Good question.

I was 2½ years older than Marietta and, as a kid, I never let her forget it. I used to brag I was much smarter than she was. She'd retaliate by announcing I was the only girl she knew who wore a concave bra.

As a teen, Marietta fell into trouble. So how could I answer Meredith's question? Breathing a quick prayer for wisdom, I answered with the first coherent thought that came to mind. "Well, Meredith, Auntie Etta has done some bad things but God still loves her."

Meredith thought about that for a moment, then said, "You mean God loves it when Auntie Etta does bad things?"

Maybe this would be harder than I thought. I reminded Meredith of the recent trouble we'd had with her whining. "Do Mama and Daddy like it when you whine?" I asked.

"No," she mumbled with downcast eyes. "Do we love you anyway?" I pressed. "Oh yes!" she quickly exclaimed.

"Well, sweetheart, it's the same with Auntie Etta," I explained. "It makes God sad when she does bad things, but God still loves her very much and He always will."

"Oh." *Silence.* "So we should love her too, right, Mama?"

In that quiet moment, Meredith grasped the Christmas story: Despite our rebelliousness, God still loves us. And He sent His Son to prove it.

Merry Christmas!
Peter and Regina Cram
Skip, Meredith, Tierney and Victoria

1997 – The Prodigal

The prodigal son. It's one of the most powerful stories ever told, and I never liked it. The younger son of a wealthy landowner greedily demanded his inheritance, then squandered it on foolishness. Starving and destitute, he headed home in shame to beg his father's forgiveness.

Overjoyed, the father threw a party to celebrate his return. The older brother, however, resented the fanfare. He'd labored for years without reward while his reckless brother got a banquet just for showing up. Where's the fairness in that? As a dutiful older sibling myself, I could relate.

Yet we recently celebrated the return of our prodigal. The funny thing is, our prodigal isn't even real; Susannah is Tierney's ragged stuffed bunny, who has a habit of wandering off when Tierney's not looking. We always found her until that terrible day she simply vanished. Susannah was on Tierney's mind every night as she fell asleep with empty arms, and every morning as she drowsily reached for her tattered friend. For months, Tierney never stopped looking and she never stopped grieving.

Then came the scream of delight when Susannah was discovered in an unused trash bin. Tierney was almost incoherent as she clutched her beloved bunny and sobbed. They danced around like lovers, spinning and laughing and kissing and weeping.

As I watched, I could picture the father running to meet his wayward son, sobbing with joy. It humbled me, reminding me again why Jesus was born among us. Yes, it was for dutiful older siblings, but also for wandering prodigals who sometimes lose their way. Until they come home, God never stops looking and He never stops grieving. And He never gives up.

Merry Christmas!
Peter and Regina Cram
Skip, Meredith, Tierney and Victoria

1998 – The Fish

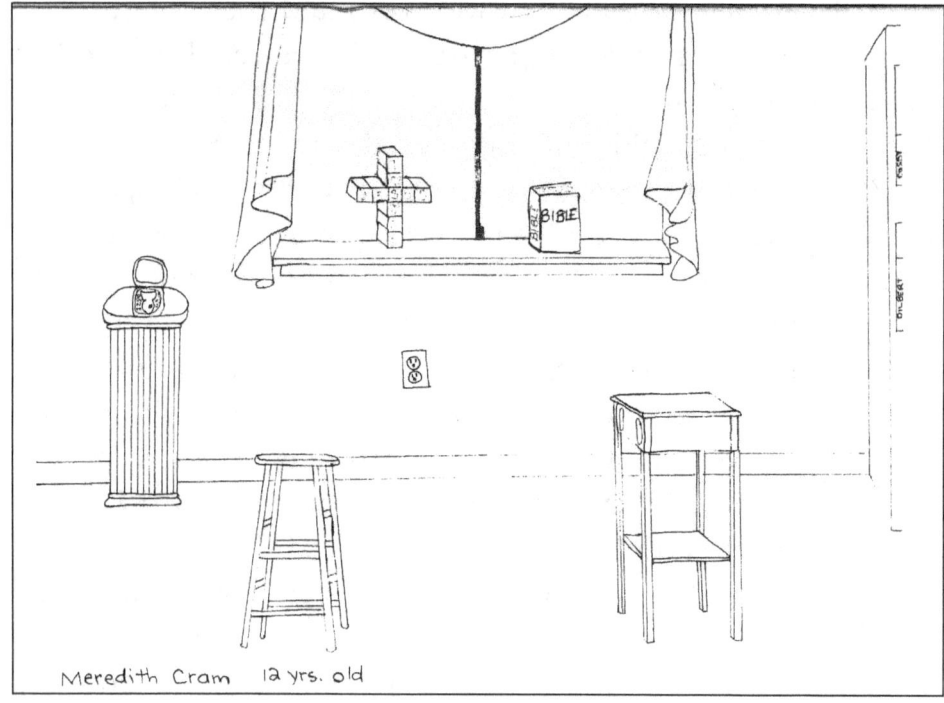

Meredith Cram   12 yrs. old

It was a wake and funeral all in one, and we couldn't stop laughing.

The mourners processed into the living room in footie pajamas, bearing the tiny jewelry-box casket where Goldie the Goldfish had been laid to rest.

We held ourselves together during the off-key rendition of "Amazing Grace" but began to lose it when 12-year-old Meredith greeted the mourners.

"Good evening," she intoned solemnly. "We're gathered to remember the fish, Gold Cram." ("*Sniff, sniff,*" I thought I heard, until a quick glance revealed Skip's impish grin.)

"Please join in prayer," Meredith continued. "Eternal rest grant unto him, O Lord, and let perpetual light shine upon him." I bit the inside of my cheeks to keep from laughing.

After another hymn, Tierney read a Bible verse about how we need fear no calamity because we've placed our trust in One who is eternal. The problem was that when she got to the word "calamity," she pronounced it more like "calamari."

Peter and Skip erupted in gales of laughter.

"We're burying a *fish,* and you're talking about *calamari!*" I choked.

Meredith shot me a dirty look.

After a few kind words about Goldie the Goldfish, the casket was carried out, then unceremoniously dumped onto the kitchen counter, where it sat for two days. As the third day dawned, rich with religious symbolism, Tierney's tears had dried, as had the fish. I insisted either she bury her long-deceased friend, or Goldie would find a permanent place in our compost heap. Thus Goldie the Goldfish was laid to rest amid the pines, marked by a simple pebble cross and two banana peels.

Surely God smiled that day as pajama-clad children came to Him, mourning their tiny friend. To such as these belongs the kingdom of God.

Merry Christmas,
Peter and Regina Cram
Skip, Meredith, Tierney and Victoria

1999 – To See His Face

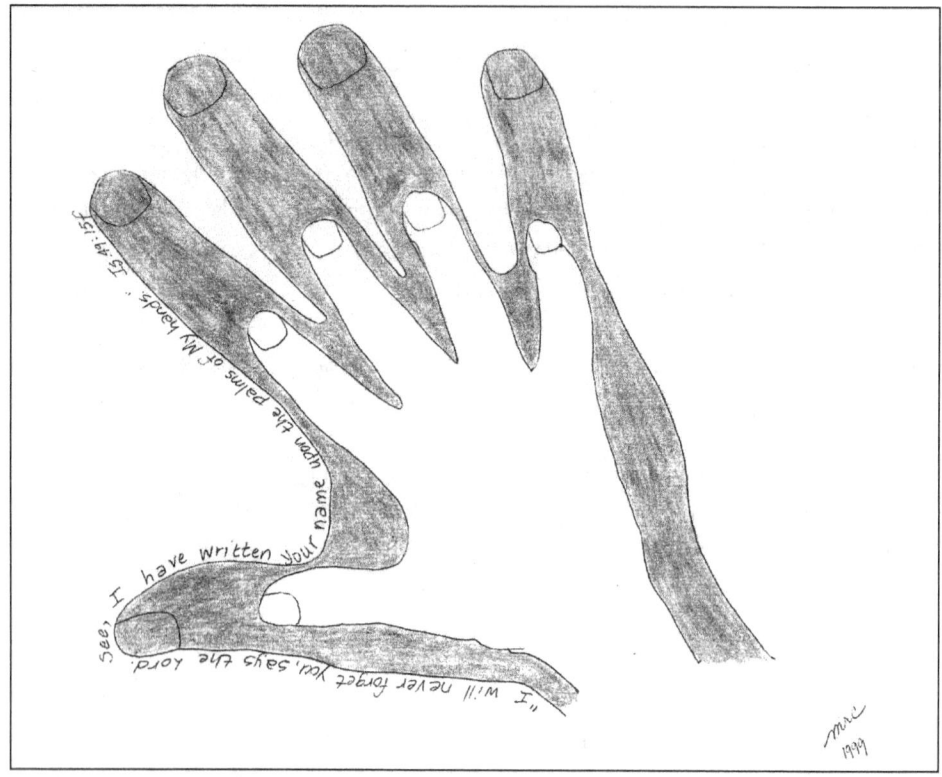

Torrie's devotion to her Daddy began well before her birth as Peter serenaded her with his gorgeous baritone voice. He'd ask about the weather and the Patriots' quarterback. Then he'd say, "Daddy loves you every day, all the time." And the baby would stir at the sound of his voice. Only his voice. No one else's.

When Torrie heard Peter's voice in the delivery room, she craned her little body toward him as though she could wait no longer to meet her beloved. Thus began one of the most remarkable love stories I've ever been privileged to witness.

As an infant, Torrie was content in the crook of his arm for hours. In return, she graced him with her first smile, her first laugh, her first baby kiss. Daddy was not just the light of her world. He *was* her world.

Unfortunately Peter had to go to work. Each morning as he drove away, Torrie would blink back tears.

And then she would wait.

One day the waiting became more than she could bear. She wiggled her way into the laundry basket, wrapped Peter's tattered nightshirt around her little body and sobbed, "Dada! My Dada!"

In desperation I cut out a small swatch of the nightshirt for her to carry around in her chubby fist. We call it her Piece of Daddy.

One evening, Torrie tripped and sliced her forehead on the raised hearth, screaming from the pain and blood. I scooped her up and placed her in her Daddy's lap, and she quieted immediately. She knew she was safe in her Daddy's arms. And all the while, her blood-stained Daddy wept because his little one was in pain.

Like that earthly Daddy, our heavenly Father cradles us in His arms when we weep.

> Peter and Regina Cram
> Skip, Meredith, Tierney and Torri

2000 – Deer Abbey

Tierney Cram Age 11 (almost 12!)

It was the week before Christmas and I was exhausted. The kids were split among three schools, the teenagers were playing sports and Peter was working 90-hour weeks in the final countdown to Y2K. (Yes, Y2K really was a thing.) I'd carpooled 600 miles that week in a dilapidated minivan that was in worse shape than I was. The windshield spritzer sprayed sideways, soaking nearby drivers. A wire held the sliding door in place so it wouldn't keep falling off, and the clock was permanently stuck at 47 minutes fast. Except during Daylight Saving Time. Then it was an hour and 47 minutes fast. I was physically and mentally exhausted – and it was my birthday.

Peter astounded me with the most unselfish birthday gift I have ever received: He sent me away alone.

I mean *really* alone, to a tiny mountain village tucked in the crook of Connecticut's Housatonic River. The Appalachian Trail winds through the nearby state forest, and the only neighbors lived peaceably in the cemetery next door. It was dark, deserted and lonely, and I loved every minute of it.

For three whole days I didn't have to referee a sibling argument. I could eat Wheaties for dinner if I wanted, and drink my morning coffee without reheating it even once. I spent untold hours pouring out my heart to God, reveling in His presence like a child who curls up on Daddy's lap simply to enjoy the pleasure of his company.

We joke that, for my birthday, Peter got rid of me. But the truth is, his gift was enormously sacrificial, modeled after the One who sent an even greater Gift to a weary and discouraged world. That Gift was the most sacrificial Gift we will ever know.

Christmas.

Peter and Regina Cram
Skip, Meredith, Tierney and Victoria

2001 – Stealing Christmas

It was Christmas week 1968 and I was a scrawny seventh-grade kid with too much time, not enough imagination and a desperate desire to fit in. Ah, the good old days.

While snooping around in my mother's closet one afternoon, I discovered a secret stash of Christmas gifts marked for us kids. The next time the house was empty, I sneaked back into the closet *(I hope my mother isn't reading this),* grabbed all the boxes marked for me and spent a delightful afternoon of juvenile delinquency. I unwrapped the Flower Power diary and lava lamp. I tried on the hip-hugger bell bottoms and fishnet stockings, preening in front of the mirror for effect. Then I carefully rewrapped my loot and returned it to the closet. *(Come to think of it, I hope my kids don't read this, either.)*

The next day at school, I was a hero. I bragged about my audacity and how I was the only kid in the small town of Swampscott to swipe all my presents. I knew it would be the best Christmas ever.

It was the worst Christmas ever. When the big morning arrived, I had to feign surprise while my parents and sisters reveled in the exchange of love. I hadn't chosen love at all; I had chosen myself – and that's exactly what I got. It turned out to be a pretty small and disappointing package.

I never did it again, for Christmas cannot be stolen, nor can it be stashed away behind flowered hats and attic stairs. Christmas can only be given away, and God in His tender mercy has done just that. He has given away Christmas, once and for all eternity.

Peter and Regina Cram
Skip, Meredith, Tierney and Victoria

2002 – Journey of Darkness

Despite the Duchess of Windsor's famous claim, it *is* possible to be too rich or too thin. I know because I've been there. Not the "too rich" part, but a year ago I stood at a skeletal 108 pounds. You could count my bones and I was so weak, the kids had to help me down the stairs. I was depressed and confused, and couldn't sleep, and we had no idea why. One day I showed up in the wrong city to pick up kids after sports practice. We laugh about it now, but at the time it was disturbing. The whole family was affected.

For years we sought answers. I was misdiagnosed and given useless drug after useless drug as I continued to descend into darkness. I finally received a startling diagnosis: I was suffering from bipolar disorder, a mental illness marked by uncontrolled mood swings thought to be caused by chemical fluctuations in the brain. After a lot of hard work and tremendous family support, I am fat and sassy again. Needless to say, Peter is breathing easier – not to mention the kids in the carpool. It's so good to hear laughter in the house again.

This is a strange topic for a Christmas card, and yet it depicts a part of our world perhaps not so very different from your own, with darkened corners and crooked lines. Perhaps, too, it is why we cherish the celebration of Christmas when God came among us to bind up the brokenhearted. This year that's precisely what He has done, and as a family we are profoundly grateful. Christmas doesn't get much better than that.

Peter and Regina Cram
Skip, Meredith, Tierney & Torrie

2003 – Roast Goober

On a sprawling hillside in the Middle East, thousands gather as a preacher stirs their hearts. Night falls and people grow hungry. A small boy makes the charming offer to share his lunchbox with the crowd. Surprisingly, the preacher agrees. He blesses the food, which feeds 5,000 people. There are leftovers. Fast forward two millennia.

It's almost dinnertime when the phone rings.

"Mom?" Meredith calls downstairs. "Is it okay if Dale comes for dinner?"

"Sure," I reply. We set an extra place at the table.

Moments later Tierney drags in from soccer. "Chelsea is eating with us," she announces.

P.J. meanders through the door and Ali stops by to say hi. We set more places and add water to the soup. As we gather to thank God for the food, Skip and Kaitlyn arrive unexpectedly.

Meredith asks to sing a new grace she learned at college. This is a kid who thinks Gregorian Chant is the coolest music ever, so I braced myself. I needn't have worried. Meredith launches into "Bless us, oh Lord, for these, thy gifts..." to the lilting tune of the *Gilligan's Island* theme song.

Peter and I silently pray for a "loaves and fishes" miracle, since the meal we planned for five must now feed 11 – most of whom are teenagers.

The kids bicker about kitchen cleanup. Torrie steals Skip's napkin. Peter regales us with Flip Wilson routines. We enter a heated debate about creationism versus evolutionism and whether they can coexist. We eat until we're full, yet the food does not run out.

Dinner draws to a close. "I love this place," Ali sighs.

So do I, and again God has graced us with His presence. May your Christmas celebration be equally blessed.

Peter and Regina Cram

Skip, Meredith, Tierney and Victoria

2004 – VW Beetle

I was minding my own business at a busy stoplight when a speeding Datsun slammed into the back of my adorable, industrial-gray minivan. No one was hurt, but the van was demolished, leaving us with only Peter's cluttered Toyota for a family with four teenagers. Peter packs half his worldly possessions just to visit the dentist, so no one was happy.

To me, the solution was obvious: replace the van with a practical car – like a Volkswagen Beetle. Convertible. In robin's egg blue. But when I broached the subject, Peter looked at me as if I'd been sniffing too much laundry detergent.

"A Beetle?" he scoffed. "One of those little bug things? How can I fit all my broken monitors in a trunk the size of a mailbox?"

I self-righteously informed him New Beetles are far better than the old ones, thank you very much. "They even have heat." Clearly I was outvoted. I grudgingly consented to the purchase of a revolting green used hatchback with a dump sticker. Did I mention it's hideous?

A few weeks later, after a delightful Christmas morning, Peter aimed a camera at me and handed me an exquisite jewelry box with a 25th-anniversary poem about how he'd marry me all over again. To be honest, I groaned. I'm not a big jewelry lover; but as he'd planned something special, I mustered my best plastic smile and opened the box.

His shutter clicked as my jaw dropped. Nestled inside was a key chain... a VW key chain. In my speechless moment, Peter explained the insurance payout from the crash had made it possible to acquire a Beetle. Convertible.

It arrived in a snowstorm. We drove home with the top down, praising God for His unmerited generosity.

It's robin's egg blue.

Blessed Christmas ~
Peter and Regina Cram
Skip, Meredith, Tierney and Torrie

2005 – Fuddy Dud

It was my turn to plan Date Night. We'd both been traveling so Peter and I hadn't seen each other in weeks. We began our date at that hotbed of romance, Bob's Discount Furniture. For years Peter had wanted an overstuffed chair. Sure enough, we found the perfect chair among the clutter of rejects at the back of the store.

Next we headed to Mass. While Peter cantored, I alternated between glorious worship and playing peek-a-boo with a nearby toddler.

Afterward, I scandalized Peter by driving to a dark, secluded section of town where we cozied up in our dilapidated Saturn wagon. I even brought blankets and pillows so we could stretch out in back. Before we got settled, however, our dark corner was illumined by a patrol car shining its headlights directly at us.

Peter was mortified. "What if he catches us?" he gasped.

"Peter, we're *married*!" I huffed, rolling my eyes.

We talked our way out of trouble and, after the law-enforcement vehicle's headlights disappeared, we thoroughly enjoyed ourselves. Then we laughed ourselves silly.

Later, at dinner, we bumped into friends and laughed some more. By evening's end, we had enjoyed worship, prayer, music, touch, laughter, friends and food. It was the perfect evening.

Not all dates are so perfect. Many have been interrupted by illness or mosquitoes or carpools. Nevertheless, Date Night is part of the glue that holds us together, along with family, laughter, and – most of all – faith. This Christmas we wish you such faith, and plenty of laughter to sweeten the journey.

Peter and Regina Cram
Skip, Meredith, Tierney and Victoria

2006 – Rapids

"Mom and Dad, I have something to tell you," Meredith began cautiously over the phone. "I'm not going back to college in the fall."

Not going back? But she loved Franciscan University of Steubenville. We didn't understand.

"I'm entering the convent," she explained.

Silence from our end.

"Mom? Dad? Are you there? I don't want to wait any longer."

Other kids call home asking for money. Ours wants to discuss the relative importance of veils.

While it's wonderful news, life is so much easier when things remain the same. I've always hated change, and nothing you say will change my narrow little mind. Skip will graduate from college in May and marry his sweetheart, Kaitlyn. Tierney is a high-school senior with plans to run away to college in the fall. Victoria is preparing to be left behind with her elderly parents. And Margee Zukas, a delightful local teen, is now part of our crazy household. Meanwhile, I'm trying to schedule a mid-life crisis, tightly squeezed between carpools and writing deadlines. Besides that, ain't nothing happening.

Back to Meredith. She did enter the convent in September. Many who heard the news expressed strong opposition. The objection that really bugged us was, "What a shame. She's such a pretty girl," as if God only uses ugly people.

It's been a sacrifice for all of us and we miss her terribly. Still, her obedience to God is inspiring.

It calls to mind another young woman centuries ago who also accepted God's invitation to obey, despite the cost. Food for thought.

Merry Christmas to all ~
Peter and Regina Cram

2007 – The Perfect Life

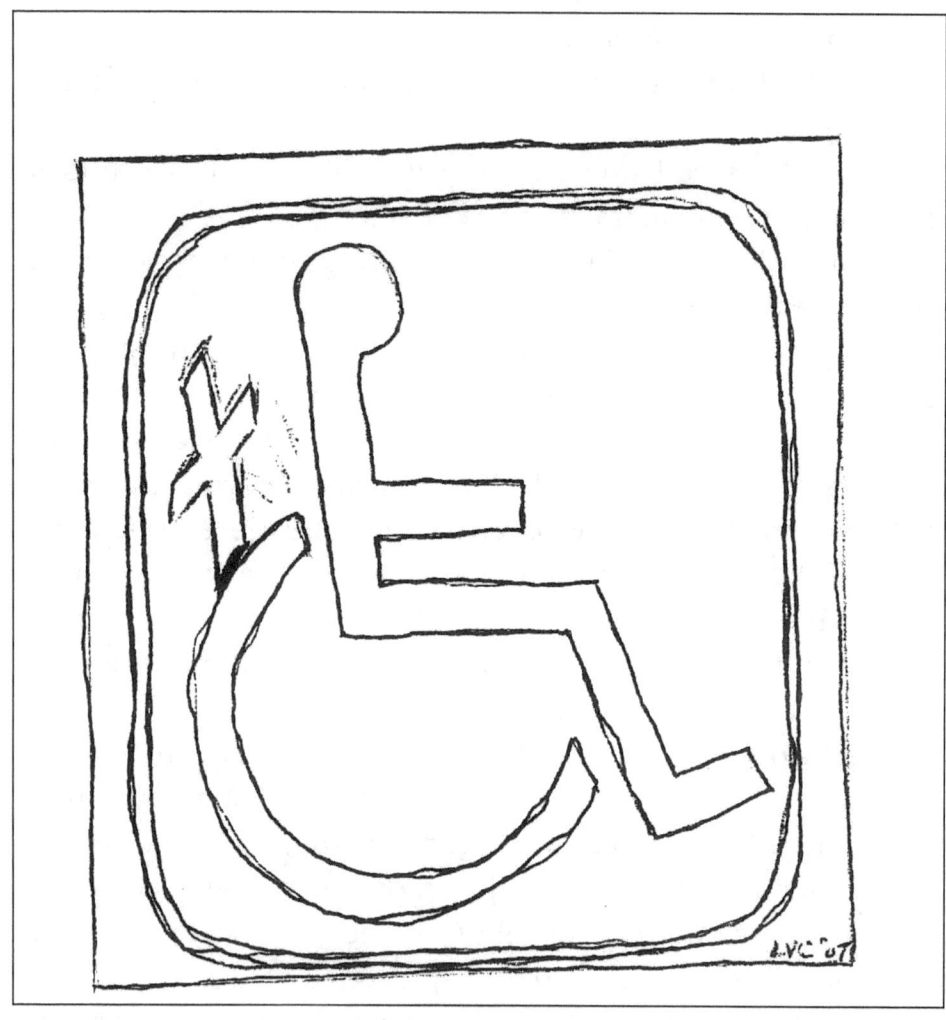

I was contemplating the Chocolate Teddy Grahams in Aisle 3 when an acquaintance stopped to chat, looking stunning as always, with perfect coif and impeccable style – a sharp contrast to my frumpy hair and jeans. After a few pleasantries, she blurted out, "You have such a perfect family."

Wait. Did she really just say that? "We're very blessed," I replied honestly, "but we have plenty of problems."

"No, you don't," she refuted me bluntly. "Your family is perfect. Your life is perfect." Yeah, right, perfect life.

I was stunned. What did she know about our lives? If life were perfect, Peter's knees wouldn't throb. I wouldn't have a mental illness...

I didn't feel I owed her an account of our troubles, but neither did I wish to be dismissed as some stained-glass saint waltzing through life on fluffy clouds. "Our lives aren't perfect at all," I asserted. "I suffer from bipolar disorder, brain damage and debilitating arthritis. We face teenage and family issues. Sometimes life is really hard."

I didn't say any more, but my internal voice continued elaborating... until my silent diatribe was interrupted by Christmas music wafting from overhead.

"Away in a manger, no crib for His bed," Bing Crosby crooned.

My mind wandered to the image of a newborn King sleeping in a dirty feeding trough. He was born to an unwed mother; a wicked king was out to kill Him; and visiting astrologers brought the gift of myrrh – which was akin to bringing embalming fluid to a baby shower. And I thought *we* had problems.

Back in Aisle 3, my acquaintance returned to her shopping, envying our perfect lives. I lingered for a moment, musing. Perhaps I've been ungrateful for the many blessings from above.

Blessed Christmas from the Crams

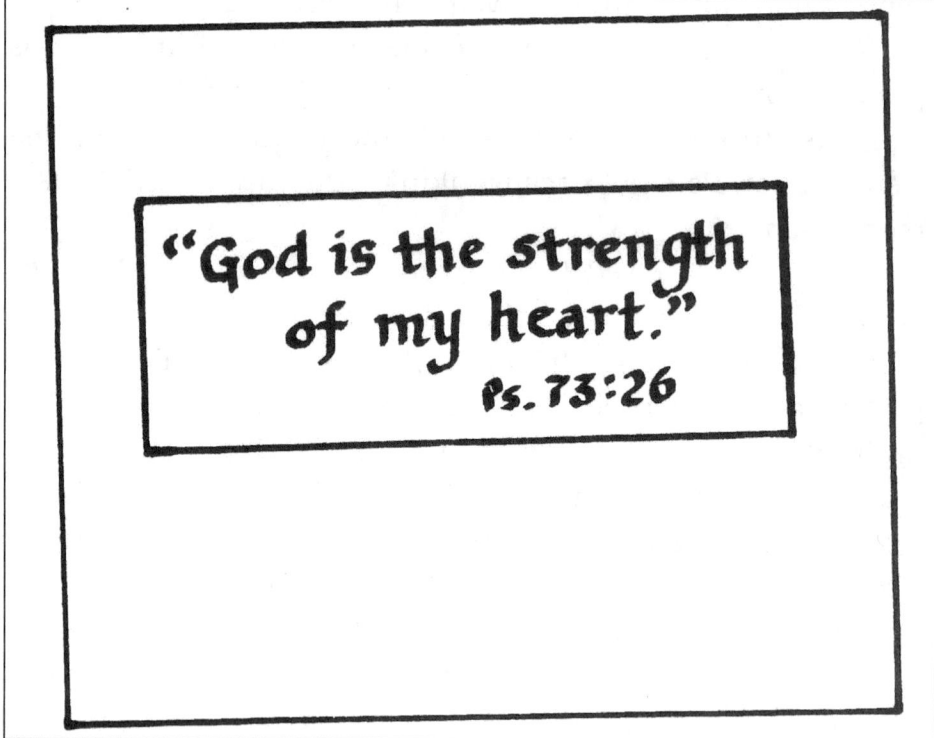

2008 – L'il Pablo

"God is the strength
of my heart."
Ps. 73:26

This has been the year of college. Skip took classes at UConn. Meredith returned from the convent and resumed college. Tierney got settled in college. Margee began college. Torrie applied to college. Peter paid bills for college.

I did laundry.

We would likely feel overwhelmed by all the tuition bills if we weren't enjoying the kids so much. And nowhere was this more evident than on our summer vacation in August.

It was our first night on Cape Cod and the seven of us had arrived – Skip and Kaitlyn, Meredith, Tierney, Victoria, Peter and me. There were kitchen-towel fights and noisy laughter and the singing of grace. Then Kaitlyn cleared her throat and we fell oddly silent. To our delight, she and Skip announced they were expecting a baby. Cheers erupted as we hugged and laughed and wept. Torrie spontaneously dubbed the baby L'il Pablo.

In an odd sort of way, it reminded me of a scene years earlier. The kids were tiny, and I was in the hospital following a catastrophic illness. Poor Peter was exhausted, so when he called me in the hospital one afternoon, I urged him to do something for himself that evening, rather than visiting me.

I could hear his voice crack on the other end of the phone. "Reg," he said, choking up, "I almost lost you. Visiting you _is_ doing something for myself."

That evening we sat together on my hospital bed and talked. We held hands, and we shared my green lime Jell-O. The grueling recuperation looming ahead was softened by our profound joy.

I suppose that's how we feel now ~ beneath hardship and uncertainty lies an unshakable joy. It is this joy we wish for you as we wait in hope for Christmas.

Peter and Regina Cram

2009 – Sir Sombrero

The phone call came at sunset: Kaitlyn was in labor, and she and Skip were heading to the hospital. Peter, Torrie and I raced to join them, panicked that we might miss the big event.

Yeah, right.

Kaitlyn's mother and Skip kept us apprised as we waited in the family lounge. Strangely, when Skip came in to deliver updates, he looked remarkably fresh and relaxed.

The hours crept by. Torrie curled up on the couch and fell asleep. Peter read. I paced. We called Meredith and Tierney, away at college. More pacing. And always we prayed.

In the wee hours of the following morning, we received the glorious news a healthy baby had been born. An hour later we were silently ushered into Kaitlyn's darkened room where a chubby newborn nestled in the crook of her arm. Skip scooped up his little one with the ease of a seasoned dad and, in that stillness before dawn, they introduced us to our first grandbaby.

I especially enjoyed watching 17-year old Torrie, who was captivated by the tiny miracle cradled in her arms. Still in her high-school uniform from the previous day, she and the baby whispered secrets and conspired against the other aunties. Now I understand love at first sight.

How is it a tiny bundle no bigger than a pot roast so thoroughly captures our hearts? But this is precisely what a baby does, bringing inexplicable joy and softening the hardships of life.

It is this joy we wish for you, as your heart is captured by the Infant of Christmas.

Peter and Regina Cram
Skip, Kaitlyn & Li'l Pablo
Meredith, Tierney & Victoria

2010 – Little Bear

The shrillness of my cell phone pierced the silence. It was Tierney, our wise 21-year-old.

"Hi, sweetheart," I answered cheerfully.

"Mom! Mom! Mom! Mom! Mom! Mom!" Tierney squealed into the phone.

I knew what she was going to say. Tierney and her boyfriend, Andrew, had been enjoying an afternoon date – a rare treat amid the demands of college and work. He'd begun the date by bringing her to an empty church. When she stepped inside, the first thing she noticed was a beautiful bouquet of red roses on a table by the door.

Once inside, Andrew got down on one knee, pulled out a small velvet box and quietly asked, "Tierney, will you marry me?"

Tierney gasped and stared at the box. "Yes!" she exclaimed.

Andrew placed the ring on her finger, then asked Tierney to take a seat in the front pew. She watched as Andrew approached the pulpit, reached behind it, and pulled out a bowl of water and a towel. He returned to Tierney, dropped to his hands and knees, removed her shoes and washed her feet.

It is the universal symbol of servanthood.

Andrew explained, "Marriage is a lifetime of service, and it's going to start with me."

This may be an odd story to share at Christmas, but then again, perhaps it's the perfect story of love and humility.

Oh, and the roses were for Tierney.

May God bless your Christmas.

Peter and Regina Cram

2011 – Ubby

Calamityware

Coffee, Please

The freak October blizzard erupted onto a Halloween land-scape. Transformers exploded. Trees crashed. Electrical wires dangled precariously.

We had just settled in for a quiet Saturday evening when the lights flickered. And then it was dark. We had no heat, no water, no electricity. Our entire town was without power.

Sunday and Monday, we worked to clear debris. By Tuesday. the inside of our house was so cold, we could see our breath. I did look rather fetching wearing a balaclava to bed.

The only thing we really missed was coffee, so on Wednesday morning, I walked two miles to the closest store with a generator, bought a pint of half & half, and walked home. I fired up our dilapidated charcoal grill, boiled a saucepan of water, and poured it over coffee grounds. It was heavenly.

By week's end, a party-like atmosphere prevailed wherever people gathered. Residents exchanged stories and offered advice. Neighbor pitched in to help neighbor, checking on the elderly and homebound.

Admittedly, it sounds more charming than it was. There's nothing romantic about being cold, or hungry, or afraid. Peter and I had it better than most because we had each other. And unlike many in the world who lack food and water, we knew our hardship would end. We had hope.

When power was finally restored, people felt a new appreciation for electricity and running water. Not me. I appreciated having hope. No matter how cold we'd been, we knew with certainty clean water and a warm home would return. It was hope that carried us through the storm. Hope, and a really good cup of coffee.

We wish you such hope this Christmas.

Peter and Regina Cram

2012 – Joy

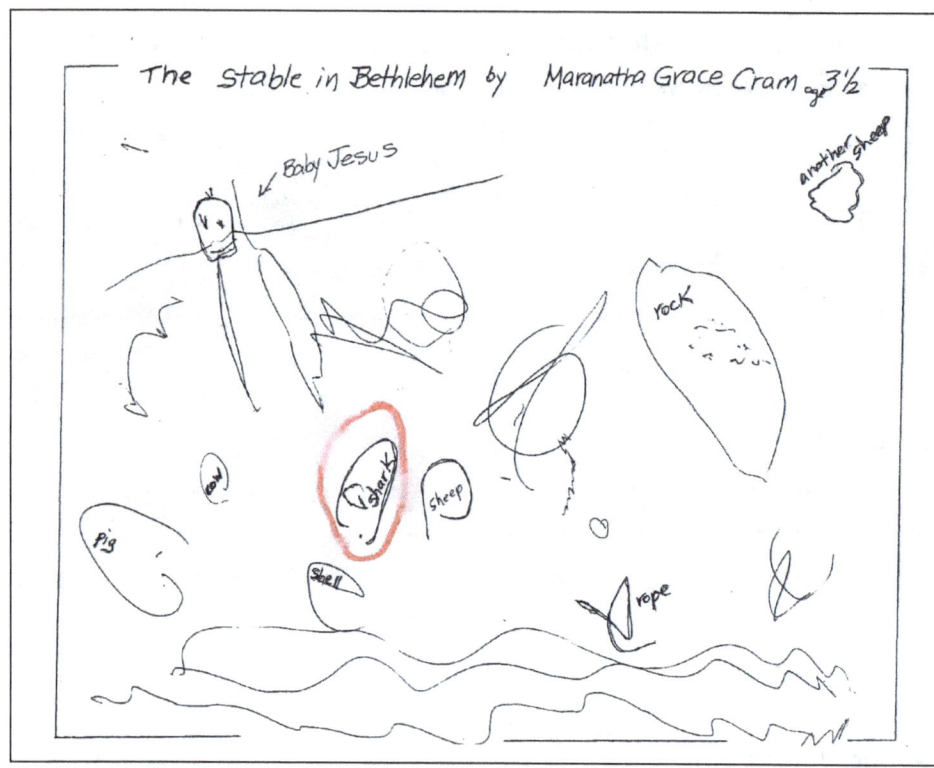

How does one admit to one's brilliant engineer husband that one is an idiot? (And by "one," I mean me.

I'd been hard at work writing a book – a compilation of some of my newspaper columns. By late September, it was almost ready to go to press.

One morning, as I fiddled with type styles and verb tenses and margin widths, my laptop started making odd sounds. That's when it occurred to me I hadn't done a file backup. Uncertain how to do it, I emailed the manuscript to Peter so he could do it for me. Rather ingenious, I thought.

My laptop began to groan. It labored. It made grinding sounds. And then it was quiet.

The manuscript never went through.

That evening, I broke the news to Peter the laptop had died.

"It was old," he said, unconcerned. "You *do* have a back-up of your work." It was a statement, not a question.

Um, about that . . .

Peter tried to retrieve the data from my lifeless machine, without success. The book was gone.

After the shock wore off, we found a replacement laptop and I began to re-create the book. I refused to feel sorry for myself – not in a world where so many people lack basic necessities. I did, however, back up my work.

Once again, the book is nearly ready. As much as we look forward to its publication, we have more important blessings. Our kids have vibrant faith and steady jobs. We have two grandbabies and two more on the way. There is love in our home. So despite my idiocy, our Christmas is filled with joy. May yours be as well.

Peter and Regina Cram

2013 – Lost and Found

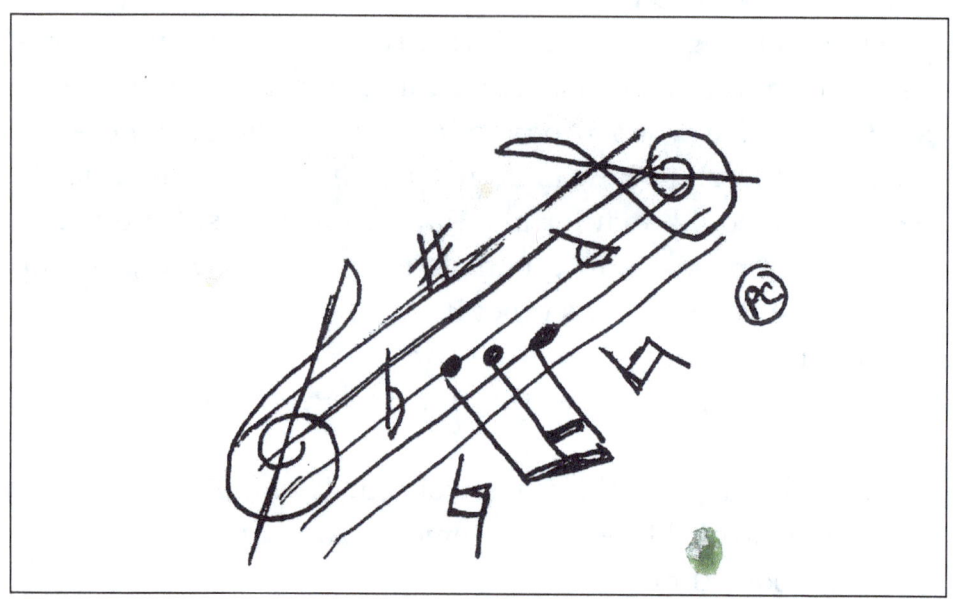

Peter and I were on Cape Cod, vacationing with our 20-something-year-old kids and their families. One night after the little ones were in bed, we gathered for an intense strategy game. Popcorn appeared, but since we didn't have vegetable oil, the kids popped it in bacon grease. It tasted even more disgusting than it sounds. Folks grabbed drinks as Skip set up the game on the porch. Everyone joined in.

Everyone except me.

A brain injury years ago makes it impossible for me to grasp the complex rules. Even a simple card game is beyond possible for me. Forget reading.

Peter hung back to keep me company until I sweetly shoved him toward the porch. He loves playing as much as the kids do, and there was no point in both of us missing out.

I curled up on the sofa with the newest grandbaby. Just seven weeks old, he made adorable sounds as he tried to talk. He grinned widely, grew drowsy from the exertion and promptly fell asleep in the crook of my arm. His soft skin smelled so sweet!

I wish I could say it took away the sting, but it didn't. It's hard to lose abilities. Given that we're heading into our older decades, we should probably get used to it.

I nuzzled my sleeping bundle as a burst of laughter emanated from the porch. We have so much for which to be grateful. Clearly, I've gained far more than I've lost. I need to remember this.

Christmas blessings to all
The Crams

2014 – Family Tree

"What's wrong with your Christmas tree, GrandMum?"

That's how our 4-year-old grandchild greeted me Christmas Day – and with good reason.

Each year Peter and the kids head to a local farm in search of the perfect tree. Each year I beg for a small one.

"Right," they say, rolling their eyes. Peter brings a rusty saw and hatchet, looking like Paul Bunyan in running tights. Thigh-deep in snow, they find a modest-size tree and hack it down. Only when they try to maneuver the blasted thing into the house do they realize their modest tree is, in fact, another monstrosity.

Last Christmas I prevailed upon Peter to cut a scraggly sapling in our yard – one that never should have taken root in the first place. It had six branches, all lopsided and droopy and pathetic. I loved it. I mean, Jesus slept in a barn; why should we need fancy?

With two quick chops of the hatchet, the sapling was down. Peter slung it over his shoulder, only to discover the trunk was too scrawny to fit in our tree stand. An inventor at heart, Peter tied fishing line to the top of the tree and suspended it from a beam on the ceiling, dangling the tree a few inches above the carpet. It did swing around, especially when the 2-year-old pushed it, but so what? How cool is it to have a swinging Christmas tree?

I'm hoping Peter will cut another sapling this year. I'd do it myself but the family fired me years ago after I brought home the most adorable Charlie Brown tree you ever saw.

Hope your Christmas is as interesting as ours.

Peter and Regina Cram

2015 – Date Night

Well, it finally happened. As of July, all four of our kids are educated, married and out of the house.

It sure is quiet.

It took me about 20 minutes to get used to the empty nest, but Peter needed some convincing. Fortunately three of our four kids live in Connecticut and all can be reached by car. In addition, Peter and I have a long-standing practice of Saturday date night, which has kept us connected through the years. A few times, when the kids were tiny and we couldn't find a sitter, I secretly (and diabolically) turned the clocks ahead; yes, date night was that important.

Nowadays, Peter and I take turns planning date night with the caveat that the other is allowed to veto the plans. This rule was established after I dragged Peter to Hartford's Bushnell Theater for a "Sound of Music" singalong, complete with patrons in lederhosen. A group of drunk revelers behind us gave new meaning to "brown paper packages tied up with string."

I'm not admitting anything, but maybe it was payback for the time Peter took me out on his 10-foot inflatable raft in the choppy waters of Long Island Sound. In pitch darkness. We had no lantern, no navigation system, no map. I get motion sickness. We got lost. It was my first time out of the house after delivering a baby.

Fortunately most of our date nights are more successful. And while the house is empty, save for the occasional invasion of kids and grandkids, it's a rich emptiness.

Quiet, yes. Lifeless, never. We wish you the same this Christmas.

Peter & Regina

2016 – Cousin Twins

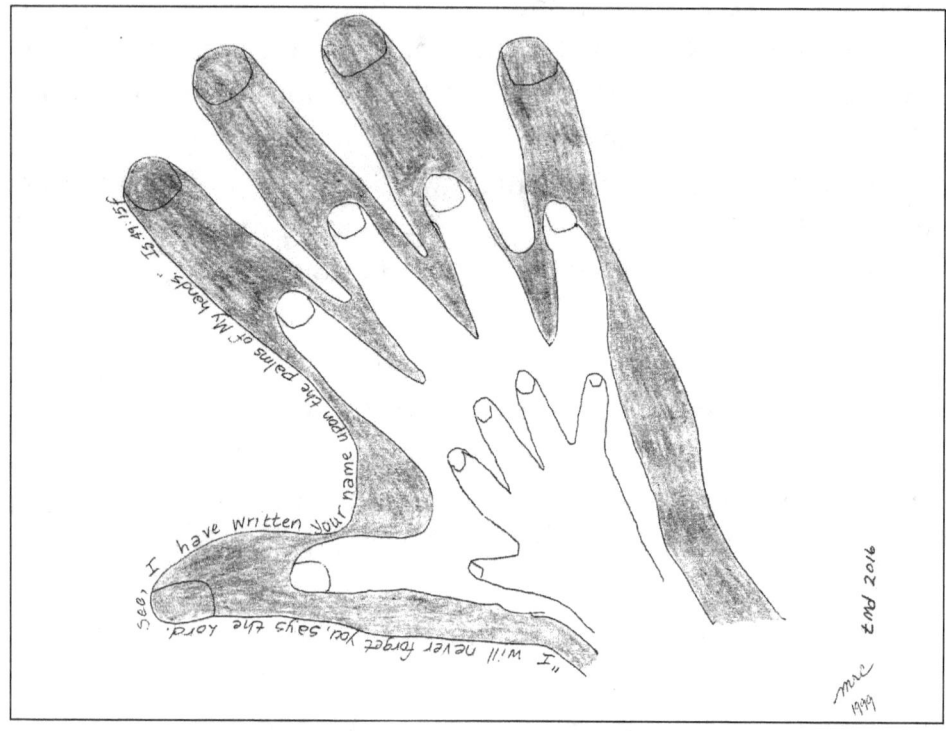

Last December our daughter Torrie and her husband Mike surprised us with a framed ultrasound picture. They were pregnant. Their baby was due August 14 in Bangor, Maine. The following week, our daughter Tierney and her husband Andrew gave us a bottle of wine from an unfamiliar winery called The First Trimester. The logo was the imprint of tiny feet. *They* were pregnant! The baby was due August 14 in Steubenville, Ohio. Despite identical due dates, I planned to attend both births. After all, it's not as if babies ever arrive on time.

On August 14, Torrie called. She was in labor and they were heading to the hospital. Peter and I raced to Bangor. An hour after our arrival, Tierney called from Steubenville to say *she* was in labor; they were heading to the hospital.

Seriously? They couldn't have planned this better?

Reluctantly, we enacted our *Let's-hope-we-don't-need-it* contingency plan. Peter stayed in Bangor while I said teary good-byes, then hopped on a plane bound for Steubenville.

My quick layover in New York turned into sweltering hours on the tarmac, due to severe weather. I grew frantic. While waiting, I learned Bangor daughter Torrie had given birth to a healthy baby girl.

At 10 p.m. they finally let us off the plane with the grim news all flights had been cancelled. I sunk my face in my hands and wept. Stranded and alone in New York, I rented a car and drove all night. Before I arrived, Tierney called with news she'd given birth to a healthy baby girl. Both babies were born on their due date, four hours apart. And I had missed both births.

Peter lingered in Bangor while I stayed in Steubenville. Then we switched.

Back home, we slept, thanking God for His tiny gifts.

Wishing you blessings of Christmas.

Peter and Regina

2017 – I Remember...

It was the morning after Christmas, and our kids watched intently as I unwrapped my birthday gift from them. It was a gorgeous wood and glass box entitled, "60 memories in honor of your 60th." Inside were 60 beautiful cards, each containing a memory.

The kids know that, years ago, I'd lost much of my long term memory and I have difficulty forming new memories. Their touching gift helped to restore some of the treasures I had lost. Their memories included:

- Listening to you read *The Hiding Place* out loud to us, curled up on the living room couch.
- Looking forward to one-on-one time with you, and Carvel sundaes with rainbow sprinkles.
- Lighting yourself on fire for our entertainment. (At Meredith's 4th birthday party, I reached across a lit birthday cake and inadvertently ignited my sweater. Her friends later told their parents, "It was so cool! Meredith's mom was on fire!")
- The time we went to the Pine Brook pool late at night (or so it seemed), just you and me.
- When you patiently endured my impatience as you taught me to drive a stick shift.
- When you taught me to make chocolate-chip meringue squares. My life will never be the same.
- That time you survived when you shouldn't have.

Our kids could have given me a sweater or the new season of "Game of Thrones." Instead, they gave their very selves in order to help make me whole.

It occurs to us a similar gift was given in Bethlehem.

Peter and Regina

2018 – More Joy

One of our most delightful family members is a kindergartner named Patrick. Patrick loves books and recess and superheroes. He gets along well with classmates and is a whiz with numbers. Nevertheless, Patrick's parents receive frequent behavior notices from school due to an unusual problem.

Patrick sings.

He sings during Circle Time. He sings in gym class and during the principal's announcements on the PA system. He sings in the library.

Patrick's singing is adorable, but it does distract his classmates. Sadly, the teacher had to inform him there would be no more singing in school. None.

It's been very hard. I mean, a man's got to sing when a man's got to sing.

Gradually Patrick has learned to keep the music inside him. One day before Christmas, however, he could no longer contain it. Standing in the middle of the boys' bathroom, Patrick burst into "Rudolph, the Red-Nosed Reindeer" at the top of his lungs. The sound reverberated off the bathroom walls into nearby classrooms. The children in those classes joined the singing as well. For one brief shining moment, music reigned.

Patrick's teacher was not happy.

We thought it was hilarious.

This Christmas, we wish you a joy that cannot be contained.

Peter and Regina

2019 – Grandbabies

It was 2 in the morning but you'd never know it by the hallway commotion. Lights blazed, metal carts rattled, the ice maker clunked noisily next door. Our daughter shifted uncomfortably in her hospital bed; our six-foot-tall son-in-law snoozed in a pull-out cot the size of a lasagna pan. I occupied the room's only chair.

We'd rushed to the hospital the previous evening, when Meredith went into labor, only to have it stall. So we waited.

Sitting in the dark, I reflected on Peter's grandpa names: Grampy Housh*, Bacca Housh, Jeepy Housh, Gampy. The little ones pretty much think he's a rock star. I wondered what this new little one would call him. Meanwhile, my mind wandered. Please, Lord, make her labor go smoothly. Do you think they'll name the baby after me? I have great child-rearing advice. Oops – bad idea. No unsolicited advice. Cram babies look like Winston Churchill. I wonder if they'll use cloth diapers. And always, please Lord, can't you give the pain to me? I cannot bear for her to endure such agony.

In the light of day, we cradled a beautiful new grandbaby. Considering our family's history with childbirth, our tears flowed freely. Grandbabies bring a depth of joy we never envisioned. We have such fun introducing them to the finer things in life, like *Star Trek* and fantasy football and diagramming sentences. And let's not forget soccer games and band concerts, all played badly. Baptisms and Saturday mornings with Grampy Housh. Toothless grins, baby kisses. We really should have had grandkids first.

We hope you will join us in our Christmas joy.

Peter and Regina Cram

* *I'd sing to our first grandchild, "Here we go to Grampy's house! Grampy's house! Grampy's house!" In her baby voice she sang, "La la la HOUSE! La la HOUSE! La la HOUSE!" So she called him House, which she pronounced "Housh." It stuck.*

2020 – Yellow Pajamas

In all our years of Christmas cards, we've never told the story of our courtship.

Peter and I met in college: he, an athletic playboy and I, a studious goody-two-shoes. One Saturday, as we rehearsed for a concert, Peter noticed my backside and decided to ask it out. Wisely keeping that thought to himself, he invited me to the local bar that evening; I declined because I was leading a Bible study. He'd heard plenty of rejection lines, but that one was new.

We finally went out on a date, and before we knew it, it was 2 a.m. "I have to go!" I exclaimed like Cinderella at the ball. "Don't you want to come to my room to see how cute my roommate looks in his yellow pajamas?" Peter smirked. I'd heard bad pickup lines, but that was the worst.

Thus our unlikely journey began. I knit him argyle socks; he cornered me in the hedges to kiss me. I told him he couldn't rent me for the evening; he crooned love songs outside my dorm to scare off other suitors. I joked that I was dating an octopus. He said it was more like dating a nun. My friends told me to ditch him.

Still, Peter was boyishly handsome, with an infectious laugh. He sang dreadful German opera and I wrote bad poetry, and we laughed until our sides ached. My friends still told me to ditch him.

During Peter's senior year, he made a decision that rocked his world. He relinquished control of his life to God. Only then did I (finally) accept his proposal of marriage.

Forty-two years have passed. Our home has been filled with extraordinary joy and devastating sorrow, but we continue to find delight in our precious calling: Marriage.

Christmas blessings to all.

Peter and Regina Cram

2021 – Real Baby

Tierney wanted a real baby and she didn't care she was only in kindergarten. By the time she was seven, her pleas had become relentless. We finally gave in, but the best we could provide was a creepy-looking doll. Tierney told everyone who would listen that the doll was a *real* baby. I honestly think she believed it. Her older brother and sister often taunted, "She's not real! She's just a big hunk of plastic!" "She's *not* a hunk of plastic!" Tierney would cry. "She's real!"

Years later when Tierney headed off to college, the creepy plastic doll remained behind, ostensibly destined for the next generation.

Well, the next generation is here. One day a group of grandkids swarmed into the house. The 4-year old made a beeline for the wooden cradle where Tierney's old doll slept. The child scooped up the doll, grabbed some baby clothes, then rushed back outside. It was as if all the fun would be sucked out of the yard if she didn't move quickly. She carefully placed the baby in our hammock, covered her with a blanket, and engineered a pull cord. Then she sat on the grass, happily swinging both hammock and baby. "*She's a real baby,*" the child confided.

Soon enough the child will outgrow that big hunk of plastic. Until then, we are patiently enduring the creepy baby doll, but loving the sweet innocence of childhood.

Maybe that's why Jesus came with the innocence of a child.

Christmas greetings,

"The leopard shall lay down with the lamb, and a little child will lead them." Is.11:6

Peter and Regina

2022 – Sacrifice

Peter and I were enjoying a delightful visit with our daughter and her family. It was autumn back home in Connecticut, but they lived in central Maine, where Mother Nature was already rushing headlong into winter.

One afternoon we took a leisurely walk along the Penobscot River until the temperature dropped and we grew cold. We were packing up to leave when I noticed a couple of teenagers huddled together for warmth. They wore just jeans and t-shirts, which weren't even close to being warm enough. I approached them and asked if they were okay.

One teen mumbled, "I'm fine."

The other quietly admitted, "Um... I'm pretty cold."

I peeled off my down vest and handed it to the girl. I'd just turned to leave when she called after me, "Wait!"

I looked back to see her outstretched hand.

She was holding my cell phone. "It was in the pocket of the vest," she explained.

This kid didn't have warm clothes to wear but she was honest enough to return a valuable phone.

When I rejoined my family, someone said something about what a sacrifice I'd made.

I stared at him. "No," I insisted. "You can't credit me with sacrifice. Giving away that vest cost me nothing. When we get home, I'll simply buy another one. Real sacrifice comes at a cost."

Real sacrifice was when Peter walked alongside me as I battled mental illness.

Real sacrifice was when my sister and brother-in-law adopted a drug-affected baby from a mother with AIDS.

Real sacrifice was how we got Christmas.

"I will not give to God a sacrifice that cost me nothing." II *Sam 24:24*

Peter and Regina Cram

2023 – Dishonesty

Last summer I stole a valuable piece of jewelry, then lied about it. I promised to look around, but I knew I wouldn't. The lies slipped off my tongue with delicious ease. The kids were horrified at my brazen fall from grace, but I'm rather proud. I'm tired of being a goody-two-shoes.

My life of crime began years ago when I bought a gold ring for a guy named Peter Cram. We married, then got busy living our happily ever after. As our 45th anniversary approached this year, I decided I would surprise him by engraving his wedding band with three small crosses. I knew he'd like it.

The only problem was how to get the ring off his finger. I stalked him for weeks before devising a plan: I'd ask him to make burgers for supper. Sure enough, Peter removed his ring to make the patties. While his back was turned, I oh-so-casually wandered through the kitchen, scooped up the ring and sleazed on my way.

Peter panicked when he couldn't find his ring. You should have seen me, masquerading as the sympathetic wife, even getting on my hands and knees to search for it. I was good.

The kids couldn't believe their eyes. "Mom!" one gasped. "You can't do that! It's just not right."

So much for teaching family values.

Ten days later, as Peter and I lingered over our anniversary dinner, I handed him a small jewelry box. He chuckled when he saw the contents, then glowered at me in horror. What kind of thieving, conniving woman had he married?! And why was she so good at lying?!

This Christmas, we wish you joy and peace. It helps if your family is more honest than ours.

Peter and "Lightfingers" Cram

2024 – Identity

Legacy

It was an idyllic summer evening as Peter and I strolled, hand in hand, through a charming New England village. We'd been married for six years, and I was finally pregnant with our first child, due in a month.

The tranquility was pierced by a distinguished-looking gentleman walking toward us. He paused, glowered at Peter and then snarled, *"You're disgusting!"* And he walked past.

We looked at each other curiously. What had just happened?

Peter was 29 years old. He wanted to look older for work so he'd grown a handlebar mustache, making him look about 35. He wore a wedding band.

I was 27 but my baby face made me look more like 20 – except, with braces on my teeth, I looked – without exaggeration – no older than 16. And because my hands had swollen, I'd removed my wedding ring.

That gentleman did not see a loving couple joyfully awaiting the birth of their first child. He thought he was looking at a 35-year-old married man who'd gotten a teenager pregnant and was strutting around town without a shred of remorse.

Things are not always as they seem. Outward signs don't always reflect reality.

Think about the Magi's gifts to the infant King. Gold signified royalty and frankincense meant the divine. But myrrh? Seriously? *As a baby gift?* Myrrh was a spice used in burial. It was akin to bringing embalming fluid to a baby shower.

But things are not always as they seem, for the Wise Men's gifts revealed the Baby's true reality.

Wishing you a wonderful Christmas.

Peter and Regina Cram

Reject #1 – Wellesley

The year was 1970. I was a skinny newcomer to Wellesley, Massachusetts. My family had moved into a modest cape-style house in a quiet neighborhood. The clothesline lent a 1950s charm, and the garden provided ample produce for the town food bank.

Wellesley had some pricey neighborhoods, but the town was generally affordable. Over the years, however, home prices skyrocketed. Just a few years ago, a neighbor put her house on the market. It was an older home in poor condition but it sold in 11 minutes, sight unseen, for nearly $1 million. The house was demolished and a mansion was erected. Right next to our little cape.

Then the day arrived when my mother and stepfather sold our home. We had hoped the new owners would appreciate its charm; but sadly, they did not. Now all that remains of our home is a hollow in the dirt. By spring, a multi-million dollar chateau will gloat in its place.

It will be handsome, but no one will remember my teenage cat is buried under the compost heap. There will be no rich harvest for the town food bank, no rotary phone with long spiral cord, no porch where five generations of Arroll women have posed.

We know we're being sentimental, but mostly we don't like throwing things away while they're still functional. We prefer to cherish them like grandparents, nurturing them well into old age, and helping them live with dignity, joy and security.

Something to think about.

Christmas blessings.
Peter and Regina

Reject #2 – Tantrum

I was heading out for special time with Tierney, our easy-going toddler. As we drove to our favorite breakfast spot, I asked Tierney, "What do you want to eat?"

"I want fen fies," (French fries) she replied cheerfully.

"Hmmm," I said. "I don't think they have French fries, but they have home fries, which are even better!"

Upon our arrival, we were escorted to a corner table, where we ordered our food. Tierney loved sitting in the booster seat. "I a bid kid!" she squealed. She chattered happily about her stuffed bunny Susannah, her sneakers that zip up the side and why she doesn't like green food.

As we began to eat, Tierney grew oddly restless. She picked at her pancake, then she began to fuss. I asked what was wrong, but by then she'd started to cry so her words were garbled.

Her tears turned to loud wails, then howls. People stared at me with that *'Why can't you control your child?'* look. I quickly realized I couldn't salvage this outing, so I scooped up my recalcitrant child along with purse, diaper bag, check and wallet.

Tierney was out of control, thrashing and shrieking. Somehow I managed to pay the bill and get us out the door. Tierney was still screaming. No one offered to help.

I had to press my no-longer-easygoing toddler into her car seat as her tantrum raged.

The screams subsided during the drive home.

As we pulled into the driveway, I asked, "What was *that* about?!!!"

Her reply was so simple. "I want fen fies."

Oh, to have life so simple that a handful of potatoes satisfies our biggest dreams. May your life be so uncomplicated as well.

Christmas blessings.
Peter and Regina

Reject #3 Sister Curly

Our daughter Meredith came tearing into this world entirely bald. I don't mean she had cute downy fuzz. She had not so much as a sprig. Strangers often asked if she was undergoing chemo.

Even as a toddler, Meredith never met a man she didn't like. She had a special penchant for grandfather types, many of whom spontaneously called her Curly, like the bald member of the Three Stooges. The nickname stuck.

She's now a talented and beautiful woman. And I'm pretty sure she's dated half the guys in the tri-state area.

So what does a girl like this do with her life?

She enters the convent.

Lest you think the convent is only for women who can't snag a husband or find a better-paying job, think again. The religious sisters I've met are funny, fascinating women.

Yet many people expressed disapproval over Meredith's decision. "You're throwing your life away!" one of them chided, as if there's a calling more satisfying than saving souls.

What really irritated us was, "What a shame. She's such a pretty girl," as if God only uses ugly people.

Nothing could be further from the truth. Consecrated life is not a cosmic booby prize; it's a life of service to which God calls special daughters.

Thus Meredith joined the Capuchin Sisters of Nazareth. May God bless you and keep you, my little one.

Postscript

After 18 months, Meredith realized while it's a beautiful life, the convent was not for her. She rejoined our noisy family and returned to school. Eventually she fell in love, got married and is now the mother of two children.

She still cherishes the time she spent in the convent.

As for us, we have profound respect for her willingness to give up everything to pursue Christ.

We love you, Sister Curly.

Reject # 4 The Wrappings of Love

Where was he?

I'd arrived at Holy Family Passionist Monastery in West Hartford in time to find good seats for the concert. Peter has a spectacular trained baritone voice, and each year he participates in concerts alongside other outstanding musicians, many of whom are professionals. Those privileged to attend are immediately drawn into worship.

The orchestra tuned, choir members filed onto the risers, and the bell choir took its place. Fr. David Cinquegrani welcomed everyone. Then he raised his baton and the first piece rang out in song.

So where was Peter?

I scanned the risers. I was searching for 5' 11", brown hair, good-looking. How hard could it be?

I searched the basses, tenors and instrumentalists. I even checked the women's sections.

Then I saw him. At least, I think it was him. It was his face, his stature and his expressions. But it couldn't be him. That guy's hair was silver, with streaks of white.

Yet it was Peter.

How is it I live with a man every day, yet fail to notice the color of his hair? Perhaps it's because when we care for someone, we cease to notice the exterior. Instead, we see the person's soul. It's like holding a treasured book whose surface we smooth with loving hands. We value the story inside, not the condition of the binding.

Such is love. We see the contents, not the wrapping, which is probably a good thing since we're rounding 60. Enjoy the contents of your Christmas this season.

Peter and Regina Cram

Reject # 5 – Miracles

Peter and I were pretty relaxed about whether our kids reached milestones at 'normal' times. This turned out to be a good thing when one of our adorable offspring was born during a life-threatening crisis. There was serious concern newborn Torrie had suffered oxygen deprivation and, hence, brain damage. Most babies who survive this rare event don't fare well.

We honestly didn't care. We loved our little dumpling, whose gentle smile lit up a room. Still, we couldn't help noticing Torrie didn't roll over, didn't crawl, didn't walk. She slept 18-20 hours a day. Even when she finally moved, she couldn't pedal a tricycle. She couldn't hold a pencil right. Her speech was garbled. A neurologist was called in.

Brain damage. That's what we thought.

At age five, Torrie cheerily headed off to kindergarten.

Not long into the school year, the teacher decreed Torrie was no longer allowed to answer math questions in class because she was so quick no one else stood a chance.

One day the teacher asked, "What's the lowest number there is?"

Predictably, the class chanted, "Zero!"

Torrie calmly raised her hand and, full of five-year-old confidence, pointed out, "My brother says there are negative numbers." She was five.

At seven she began reading *Lord of the Rings* while curled up with her Barney pillow. She hit the Terrible Twos when she was nine, making her more sophisticated at finding ways to torment us.

Torrie graduated from college summa cum laude. Don't even think of debating her on economic policy.

So maybe it's time for us to stop worrying about brain damage. Oh, and now she rolls over just fine.

This Christmas, join us in celebrating the miracles in your life.

Reject # 6 – Chittenden

It was Veterans Day and the living room was littered with wrapping paper. At the conclusion of the gift giving, I handed Peter his final birthday gift – an invitation to go away with me in January to the remote village of Chittenden, Vermont. Peter was turning 60, so a celebration seemed fitting.

There was a momentary pause. Then one of the little ones called out, "Wait! There's one more gift for Gwampy Houth*," he lisped.

Peter looked up questioningly as the child toddled over to him with an empty basket.

A second child handed him a crumpled piece of paper that read, "Me too! Me too!"

Not understanding, Peter placed it in the basket.

Meredith gave Peter a note that said, "Are we there yet?"

Other notes read, "Oooh Oooh! Pick me! Pick me!" and "How do you spell Chittenden?" and "Can my imaginary friend come with us?"

It took a few clues before Peter put it together. This was not a romantic getaway for the two of us. We were *all* going to Chittenden – all 15 of us, including our kids and spouses, a bonus Cram and all the grandchildren.

After we bushwhacked our way through endless miles of treacherous dirt and icy roads to Chittenden, our frigid stay was delightful. We raced through sub-zero temperatures in bare feet to jump into the hot tub. The most recently married couple scored what we dubbed the "Honeymoon Suite," off the garage. We played board games until we got to laughing too hard to continue. Everyone went home with a t-shirt that read, "Housh Party."

We wish you such joy this Christmas and beyond.

*Peter's grandpa name

Reject # 7 – More Hands~On Creche

It was a few days before Christmas and our young grandson was helping us set up the creche.

"GrandMum?" he asked sweetly. "Where's that guy who lives with Mary? And where's Baby Jesus?"

Sure enough, Jesus and Joseph were missing.

During our kids' teenage years, Jesus often disappeared. I think the kids were just messing with us. We usually found Him hiding in the bottom of someone's Christmas stocking, but one year we couldn't find Him anywhere. Not wanting to be without Baby Jesus on Christmas morning, Torrie found a smooth white rock to take His place. Jesus eventually showed up, but we couldn't bring ourselves to throw away the rock. It seemed a tad sacrilegious.

In ensuing years, Jesus disappeared and reappeared several times. When we sold the house seven years ago, we found Jesus at the bottom of the dehumidifier. Joseph turned up in a basket of cloth diapers. Newly missing this year, however, are a shepherd and two wise men. The camel has a broken leg. We still have the rock.

This Christmas, it's just Peter and me in the house, so we can't claim the kids are messing with us. But we know one thing for certain: Buying a hands-on creche was one of the smartest and most entertaining things we've ever done. Pretty sure God has enjoyed the antics as well.

Merry Christmas!

Reject # 8 – Rules? What Rules?

My mother believed rules didn't apply to her, and nowhere was this more apparent than in her driving. When I was growing up, Mom once jammed 13 kids into her Beetle convertible for a drive to the beach. Safety was never one of her top concerns, but she did instruct us how to dive to the floor of the car if we spotted a police officer.

My mother parked in front of fire hydrants and drove the wrong way up one-way Boston streets. Take a deep breath here, but growing up, Mom cut the seatbelts out of our cars because they shackled her freedom. That's how we were able to dive to the floor of the car so quickly when we saw police.

Mom once bought illegal fireworks from the Mafia – and paid for them by check! At age 94, she resisted using a walker because she said it wasn't a good look for attracting a husband.

Mom frequently invited odd assortments of guests to Sunday dinner. One week there might be single mothers and gay guys and the recently divorced. She often included refugees who were struggling to learn English or navigate the bureaucracy of the Registry of Motor Vehicles. Over the years, Mom reached out to a quirky assortment of lonely people who reveled in home-cooked food, lively discussion and the offer of friendship. At the lowest times in her life, she filled her home with people who were hurting even more than she was.

As you celebrate Christmas, join us in giving thanks for the eccentrics among us. They make our world so much richer.

Reject #9 – New Life

Fifteen years ago Peter and I were lingering over dinner when we began talking about downsizing. I grabbed a paper napkin and sketched the floor plan of my ideal small home. Unfortunately, I have the artistic talent of an Oreo, so my drawing looked less like a blueprint and more like the diagram of a complex football play.

Peter's top priority was living above the 500-year flood mark. What can I say? He's into weather. He also wanted air conditioning, which didn't make my list at all. I wanted minimal outdoor work and a lot of windows.

Later that evening, our 17-year-old added to the list: hot tub, ocean view (we're 40 miles from the shore), trampoline room and the original Mona Lisa.

Years passed and we continued to think and pray about moving. The day finally arrived when Peter pulled one weed too many; so, with many hurrahs from my corner, we put our house on the market. We bought a small place on a sleepy lane that's walking distance to downtown. It does have A/C; but, alas, neither ocean view nor Mona Lisa.

Despite our teary good-byes to the homestead where we raised our family, we love our new place. We have a climbing tree with a hammock, and a cul-de-sac where the little ones can play without fear. It's all on one floor and we don't have to rake leaves. And best of all, Dunkin' Donuts AND Daybreak Coffee Roasters are just 952 steps away. (Yes, we counted.)

We're in a new season of life. We still have Legos and wooden trains and Dr. Seuss books everywhere, but it's no longer our kids playing with them; it's *their* kids. Words can't express our joy.

Blessings this Christmas

Reject # 10 – The Rock

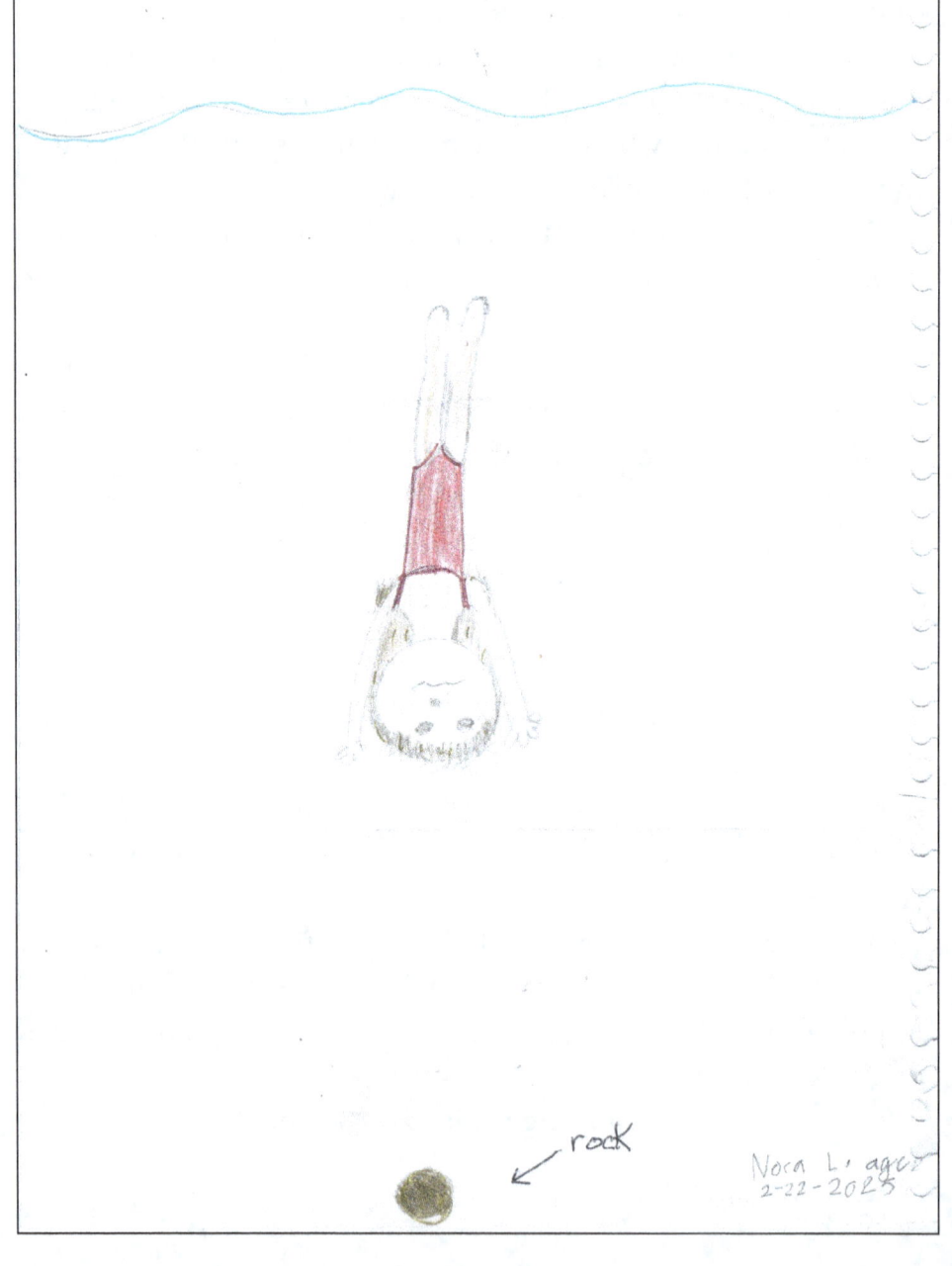

rock

Nora L. age
2-22-2025

It began like any normal conversation – as normal as it gets in our house, anyway. Our dinner guest turned to the children and inquired about their activities and passions.

"Soccer!" a middle child cried out.

"I like to read!" replied another.

"I play basketball and we all swim at Pine Brook in the summer," explained our eldest. "It's a pool down the street."

"*I'm scared about the rock!*" seven-year-old Torrie erupted without explanation.

"The *rock*?" our guest inquired with a grin.

"I'llneverbeabletopickuptherocksoI'llneverpassLevelseven andI'llhavetotakeswimminglessonsfortherestofmylifeandI'll betheonlykidinsecondgradewhocan'tswiminthedeepend!" she cried, all in one breath.

It was hard not to laugh.

Her brother explained to our guest that, in order to pass Level 7 swim class, swimmers must retrieve a rock from the bottom of the deep end of the pool. Torrie was only in Level 4 but she'd already worked herself into an Olympic-sized tizzy.

"What if I get partway to the bottom and can't swim any further? What if I get to the bottom and run out of breath? What if I get down there but can't find the rock? What if the rock is too heavy to pick up? What if I can only swim part way back up?"

"*Then drop the rock!*" her siblings hollered in unanimous exasperation.

"Torrie, what do you think will happen when you get to heaven?" I mused. "I wonder if God will say, 'Gee, I'm not sure I can let you in. I mean, did you ever get that rock in Level 7?'"

God tells us to build our lives upon the Rock. I don't think that's the one He had in mind.

Christmas blessings.

Reject #11 – Almost

Caution: This story contains the description of a near-drowning.

Each summer, Peter and I love to swim at a local pool. One day, while swimming laps, I sucked in a huge gulp of water that went down my windpipe. I began coughing so violently I couldn't keep swimming. I knew I had to get to the shallow end where I could stand, so I sank to the bottom in order to push off and propel myself forward. But the pool was deeper than I expected and I inhaled more water, further flooding my lungs. I clawed my way to the surface, gasping for air, but my lungs were full of pool water and I kept being pulled under, against my will.

I tried calling for help, but if you can't breathe, you can't speak. My lungs burned in a frantic need for air. I had exhibited nine of the ten signs of a real drowning.

Just then, a young woman approached the lifeguard. Pointing to me, she said, "I think that lady might need help."

The lifeguard seemed surprised, but she asked me, "Do you need help?"

I tried to nod. Then my eyes rolled back in my head, and I went under for the last time.

All hell broke loose as lifeguards sprang into action. They carried me to the shallow end and sat me on the steps as I gasped for air. Everyone was watching. I was so embarrassed. I wanted to tell people I'm a good swimmer, but under the circumstances, it would have sounded ridiculous.

I gagged and choked for days.

No words can express our gratitude for the young woman who saw something, so she said something. And we thank God for another breath, another tomorrow, another Christmas.

Peter didn't think a story about drowning was appropriate for a Christmas card. Go figure.

Reject #12 – Cherishing

It was the night before Mike and Torrie's wedding, and the dads were making speeches.

"Mike," Peter began, "I'm here to give you fair warning about what you're getting yourself into."

Laughter rippled through the small crowd.

"It began in 1990," Peter continued. "I was happily married with three great kids. Then one night in a bar, I found out we were going to have another baby. *(Yeah, in a bar.)*

"I was the first person to gaze into Torrie's eyes, the first to hold her in my arms and tell her she's smart and beautiful and we love her. In return, she graced me with her first giggle, her first word, her first baby kiss.

"One day when she was 5, Torrie announced she wanted to marry me. She tried to be brave when I explained she couldn't marry me because I'm already married. A few days later, she presented her back-up plan: She would marry her big brother, Skip. Mike, I'm afraid that makes you her third choice."

More laughter.

"You and Torrie have known each other a long time, Mike, but there are some quirks we think you should know about. Are you aware she's terrified of bunny rabbits? Do you know she won't swim in Cape Cod Bay because she's afraid of being attacked by minnows and crabs? And yet she'd run into a burning building to save a friend. Probably a stranger. Possibly even a bunny.

"Tomorrow, Mike, I'm giving you the most precious gift I have to offer. And as I do, I hope you won't mind if I make one request: *Cherish her.*

"It's the only thing I'll ever ask of you.

"Just cherish her."

Christmas blessings to all.
Peter and Regina

www.ingramcontent.com/pod-product-compliance
Lightning Source LLC
Chambersburg PA
CBHW071333130626

46556CB00004B/1875